BRITISH RAILWAYS

PAST and PRESENT

No 37

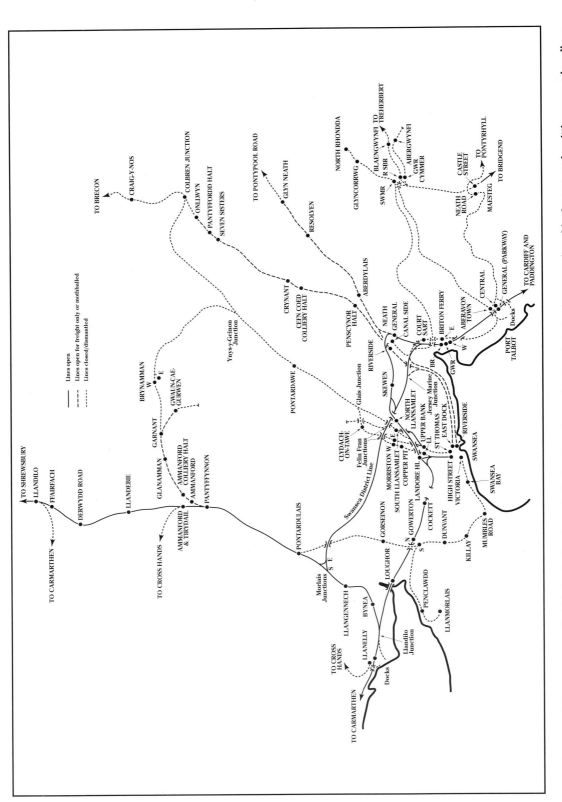

Simplified map of the area covered by this book, showing only the locations featured in the photographs or mentioned in the text, and omitting some minor lines.

BRITISH RAILWAYS
PAST and PRESENT

No 37

South Wales
Part 3: West Glamorgan and the Brecknock and Carmarthen county boundaries

Terry Gough

Past and
Present

Past & Present Publishing Ltd

First published in 2002

British Library Cataloguing in Publication Data

A catalogue record for this book is available from the British Library.

ISBN 1 85895 162 3

Past & Present Publishing Ltd
The Trundle
Ringstead Road
Great Addington
Kettering
Northants NN14 4BW

Tel/Fax: 01536 330588
email: sales@nostalgiacollection.com
Website: www.nostalgiacollection.com

All tickets and other items of ephemera are from the author's collection.

Printed and bound in Great Britain

BIBLIOGRAPHY

Barrie, D. S. M. *A Regional History of the Railways of Great Britain, Volume 12 South Wales* (David St John Thomas, 1994) ISBN 0 946537 69 0

Clinker, C. R. *Register of Closed Passenger Stations and Goods Depots* (Avon-Anglia Publications & Services, 1978) ISBN 0 905466 19 5

Cooke, R. A. *Track Layout Diagrams of the Great Western Railway and BR Western Region, Sections 50A, 51 to 56* (Author, 1982-96)

Gatehouse, Don and Dowling, Geoff *British Railways Past and Present No 28, South Wales Part 2* (Past & Present Publishing, 1995) ISBN 1 85895 084 8

Gough, Terry *British Railways Past and Present No 38, West Wales* (Past & Present Publishing, 2002) ISBN 1 85895 175 5

Hands, Peter *BR Steam Shed Allocations – Western Region Sheds (Part 3)* (Defiant Publications, 1985)

Hale, Michael *Steam in South Wales, Volume 2 North and West of Swansea* (OPC, 1981) ISBN 86093 152 8

Steam in South Wales, Volume 3 Main Line and the Docks (OPC, 1981) ISBN 86093 169 2

Steam in South Wales, Volume 6 The General Scene (Welsh Railway Research Circle, 1999) ISBN 0 9527267 2 6

Hale, Michael and Miller, Tony *Steam in South Wales Series Index* (The Wider View, 1999) ISBN 0 9535848 0 1

Heart of Wales Line Guide (Heart of Wales Line Travellers Association, 1999) ISBN 0 9536691 0 6

Jones, G. B. and Dunstone, D. *Origins of the LMS in South Wales* (Gomer Press, 1999) ISBN 1 85902 676 1

The Vale of Neath Line (Gomer Press, 1999) ISBN 1 85902 446 7

Page, James *Forgotten Railways of South Wales* (David & Charles, 1988)

Siviter, Roger *Past & Present Companion: The Central Wales Line* (Past & Present Publishing, 1999) ISBN 1 85895 138 0

British Railways Past and Present No 32, Mid Wales and the Marches (Past & Present Publishing, 1998) ISBN 1 85895 137 2

Smith, Paul *The Handbook of Steam Motive Power Depots, Volume 2* (Platform 5 Publishing Ltd, 1989) ISBN 0 906579 95 3

CONTENTS

ACKNOWLEDGEMENTS

Thanks are due to the several photographers who willingly loaned their work. I am particularly grateful to Don Gatehouse, who provided material that he had gathered during the preparation of other 'Past and Present' books covering South Wales. Some of the closed stations are now in private hands and I am grateful to the owners for granting me permission to take photographs. I thank Mr Christopher Rees of Cefn Coed Colliery Museum, Mr Rob Merrill of the Neath Museum & Art Gallery, and Mr Peter Bennett of the Collections Centre of the National Museums & Galleries of Wales, for providing information and archive photographs. I also thank Ray Caston of the Welsh Railways Research Circle for checking and making additions to some of the captions. Wales & West Passenger Trains and First Great Western provided current train timetables and First Cymru the bus timetables!

BRITISH RAILWAYS (W)   S.77
SWANSEA H.ST A
PLATFORM TICKET 1d
Available ONE HOUR on DAY of ISSUE ONLY
NOT VALID IN TRAINS, NOT TRANSFERABLE
To be given up when leaving Platform
FOR CONDITIONS SEE BACK

9896

ABERGWYNFI is seen on 14 May 1954, with the 12.35pm Bridgend push-pull train hauled by 45XX Class No 5555. The line to Abergwynfi goods and Avon Colliery runs at the rear of the platform. The site, now overgrown, is seen almost 40 years later. *John Edgington/Geoff Dowling, both courtesy Don Gatehouse*

INTRODUCTION

The railway network of Glamorgan was complex and its origins lay in the desire of competing railway companies to reach the coalfields and docks. The lines of different companies were sometimes built almost in parallel, dictated in part by the terrain; it was obviously easier to build along the valleys. There was a huge amount of coal traffic and, increasingly, industrial products such as iron, steel and chemicals. There was also a heavy passenger demand, both for local and long-distance travel. As always, some lines became financially unsustainable and much of the duplication was eliminated by closures.

I have arranged the book as far as possible by starting from Swansea along the lines of each railway company, covering first the lines heading east and lastly those to the west. I have only covered lines that became part of the Great Western Railway (GWR) or the London Midland & Scottish Railway (LMSR), and later British Railways (BR). I have not included the many private lines, for example those owned by the National Coal Board and its predecessors. I have used the placename spellings as in the Western Region Passenger Services Timetable of September 1961, or earlier where stations had already been closed. I have also identified the railway company against each station in the Index of Locations; since many towns had more than one station I have given the post-Grouping or Nationalisation name as appropriate.

The main line from Chepstow and Cardiff, through Neath to Swansea, opened in 1850. The line from Landore (a mile north of Swansea High Street) to Carmarthen opened in 1852, but there was no direct link from High Street to Carmarthen until the Swansea West Loop was opened in 1906. Swansea High Street station was modernised in the 1920s and again in the 1984, but it remains a terminus and trains from the Cardiff direction still reverse here before proceeding further west. The main-line station at Neath is conveniently located in the town. It has been rebuilt or modernised several times, the last occasion being in the 1990s. By 1964 only Bridgend, Port Talbot and Neath stations remained open between Cardiff and Swansea, but in the early 1990s new stations were opened on the main line at Briton Ferry, Baglan, Skewen and Llansamlet, none on the sites of the original stations. Llansamlet is half a mile east of the previous station (Llansamlet North, closed in 1964) and Baglan Sands (closed in 1939) was on the adjacent Rhondda & Swansea Bay (RSBR) line. All these new stations have through trains to London Waterloo!

The traffic converging on the Swansea area from the numerous industrial sites by the end of the 19th century resulted in congestion, so the GWR built a new line (between Skewen and Llandilo Junction) that enabled through trains from the east to Llanelly and beyond to avoid Swansea; another major impetus was the opening of Fishguard Harbour. This new line had the added attraction of being less steeply graded than the line via Swansea; opened in sections between 1912 and 1913, it was referred to as the Swansea District Line. Another new line (between Dynevor Junction and Jersey Marine Junction North), referred to as the Neath Loop and joining the District Line, was opened in 1915. These two lines are still open.

Swansea East Dock was served by the GWR to Neath along the Vale of Neath (Cwm Nedd). There was an adjacent station (Riverside) on the RSBR, for Blaengwynfi and Blaen Rhondda via Aberavon, with a short branch to serve Neath. Alterations in the Port Talbot area in the 1930s enabled part of the RSBR line to be closed, trains using the GWR main line to Swansea High Street. Riverside closed in 1933 and East Dock station in 1936. The GWR Cwm Nedd line lost its passenger service in 1964, but remained open for coal traffic to Cwmgwrach (Glyn Neath) until April 1999. There is now an aggregates and coal depot at Cwmgwrach, with several trains per week.

Neath was also served by the Neath & Brecon Railway (NBR), whose line ran along the

Dulais Valley, initially to Onllwyn in 1864, later extended to Brecon. The line closed to passengers in 1962 and to freight beyond Onllwyn in 1963. It was re-opened for slate traffic from Craig-y-Nos the following year, but was later cut back to Onllwyn, which remains open.

From Port Talbot, the Port Talbot Railway (PTR) opened its passenger service to Maesteg and Pontyrhyll in 1898, extending to Blaengarw (GWR) in 1902. Passenger services were cut back to Maesteg in September 1932 and withdrawn over the remaining section to Port Talbot the following year. Freight traffic continued until August 1964. The PTR also had other lines, south-east to Tondu and north-east along the Avan Valley (Cwm Afan)

The South Wales Mineral Railway (SWMR) from Briton Ferry joined the Avan Valley and ultimately ran along the Corrwg Valley. It was built mainly for the transport of coal and ran miners' trains only between Cymmer Corrwg and North Rhondda until 1961.

Apart from the GWR, other major companies were keen to have access to Swansea. The Midland Railway had a line from Colbren Junction along the Swansea Valley to its station of Swansea St Thomas; it also had a branch to Brynamman, opened in 1864. The Midland route closed to passengers in 1950. However, part of the old Midland line has been re-opened for passengers and is currently operated as a leisure line by the Swansea Vale Railway, founded in 1985.

The London & North Western Railway (LNWR) reached Swansea from Shrewsbury via Llandilo and named its terminus Swansea Victoria. Between Llandilo and Pontardulais the LNWR had running powers over the GWR line (to Llanelly). The LNWR section from Pontardulais to Victoria opened in December 1867, with a branch from Gowerton that reached Llanmorlais in 1884. The branch closed to passengers in January 1931 and completely in September 1957. The LNWR main line closed to passengers between Pontardulais and Swansea Victoria in June 1964 and passenger trains were diverted to Swansea High Street, with a reversal at Llanelly. The line was kept open for coal traffic from Pontardulais to Gorseinon until 1974, when a new link line was built to connect Gorseinon to the Swansea District Line. The Shrewsbury to Swansea line is now referred to as the Heart of Wales Line and it is promoted by a travellers' association. In addition to the four trains each way per day on weekdays (one on Sundays), there are occasional steam- or diesel-hauled special trains. The GWR line between Llanelly and Llandilo had opened in stages between 1839 and 1857. There was a branch to Garnant (opened in 1840) and Brynamman (opened 1842). From Garnant there was also a line to Gwaun-cae-Gurwen and later further south through Cwmgorse. The Brynamman branch closed to passengers in 1958, but was retained as far as Garnant (and to Gwaun-cae-Gurwen) for coal traffic until April 1999; it is currently mothballed. The GWR had a short branch from Tirydail to Cross Hands. Another line to reach Cross Hands (a different station) was that of the Llanelly & Mynydd Mawr Railway (LMMR) from Llanelly, which was built for the carriage of coal. It closed completely in 1989.

In preparing this book, I have covered all the open passenger and freight lines by train, although of necessity I used a car for the closed lines. I also used local buses, and for 'past' visits used a bicycle. Such an undertaking is never straightforward and this book in particular has had more than the usual difficulties. Most of the present-day photographs were taken during restrictions because of foot and mouth disease, thus barring access to some sites. Another unexpected constraint was the permanent banning of pedestrians from several of the new main roads in Glamorgan, some of which are on old trackbeds. A difficulty in matching some of the past and present views, which must be unique to South Wales, is that mountains have been moved in the intervening period! Many of the mining areas have been subject to land reclamation schemes over the past few decades and these have completely transformed the backdrop to many railway locations. An unwelcome hazard has been vandalism, experienced by both the railway companies and the author himself.

The weather is of course unpredictable. What was encouraging was the almost universal welcome wherever I went, both by railwaymen, the owners of private property and the general public. For this I am most grateful.

Terry Gough
Sherborne, Dorset

Swansea High Street towards Cardiff

SWANSEA HIGH STREET (1): The end of the line – 'Hall' Class No 5913 *Rushton Hall* **stands at the buffer stops at Swansea High Street after working a long-distance passenger train on 30 April 1960. The tail lamp is in position on the buffer beam ready for the locomotive to reverse out to Landore Locomotive Depot.**

On 9 September 2000 Class 150 No 150234 is at the stops forming the 08.45 from Cardiff. The train is allowed 5 minutes at Swansea before continuing to Milford Haven. *John Hodge, courtesy Don Gatehouse/TG*

SWANSEA HIGH STREET (2): At the London end of the station on 3 April 1964 is 94XX Class pannier tank No 8414. In the background is Hafod Yard.

The semaphore signals disappeared in the MAS scheme of the 1970s and the area is now controlled from Port Talbot panel box. On 9 September 2000 the Milford Haven train is seen leaving after reversal. On the left is a London-bound train that had left Carmarthen at 09.34. *Jack Hodgkinson/TG*

SWANSEA HIGH STREET (3): The main station building, seen first in the 1960s, is still in use and the entrance has been improved with the addition of trees and shrubs, as seen in September 2000. *Linden Stone/TG*

SWANSEA HIGH STREET (4): 8 June 1961 saw the last steam-hauled up 'South Wales Pullman', which was worked by 'Castle' Class No 4090 *Dorchester Castle*. While this was a sad occasion for steam fans, the locomotive is in the well-cleaned condition typical of Landore Depot's top link engines.

In the same platform on 9 September 2000 is another Paddington train, this time with Class 43 No 43017 on the front and 43035 on the rear. An hourly service is provided to London, even on Sundays. *Hugh Ballantyne/TG*

SWANSEA HIGH STREET (5): A freight train from Hafod Yard approaches High Street on 30 April 1960 behind 57XX Class No 9761. The line along the side of the platform being used by the freight train led to North Dock, but has since been removed and the land used as a road and car park.

High Street yard is still in use for the berthing of passenger stock and for the Royal Mail trains, one of which can be seen in the background on 20 September 2001 as Class 150 No 150247 enters Swansea, where it will terminate, forming the 13.50 from Fishguard Harbour. *John Hodge, courtesy Don Gatehouse/TG*

LANDORE HIGH LEVEL (1): A special train bound for West Wales approaches Landore from Swansea High Street on 25 September 1965; the engine is 'Grange' Class No 6859 *Yiewsley Grange*.

Several of the lines have since been taken up and buildings demolished, but the location is identified by the stone wall and houses. Swansea High Street station is just visible in the background. *Mike Vinten/TG*

LANDORE HIGH LEVEL (2): The station was at the northern apex of a triangle formed by the lines from London, Swansea and Carmarthen. Brush Type 4 diesel No D1671 (later Class 47) passes the station on a down express on a wet 25 July 1965; the engine was withdrawn in April 1966. The station had closed the previous November, depriving the town of its second station. Landore Low Level, on the line between Swansea High Street and Morriston West, had closed at the beginning of 1954.

Another wet day greeted the photographer in September 2000, when he found the site completely cleared. Note the two chimneys on the horizon and the buildings on the right below the embankment, which help align the two photographs. *F. Hornby/TG*

LANDORE LOCOMOTIVE DEPOT was within the triangle of lines. The depot closed in June 1961 and has been replaced by a diesel depot, and this is the view from the south side in the 1950s and 2001. The circular brickwork that protects a fuel tank in the bottom right-hand corner is virtually on the site of the turntable. The Swansea to London main line is on the right and the Swansea to Carmarthen line behind the camera. *Linden Stone/TG*

LANDORE DIESEL DEPOT is seen here on 25 July 1965. The depot is still open, but nothing was outside on the afternoon of 19 September 2001. *F. Hornby/TG*

NEATH GENERAL (1) was the town's main-line station, situated near the town centre. 51XX Class No 4110 approaches Neath on the 11.00am from Pontypool Road on 3 April 1964.

The loop and goods yard to the right have both been removed and the land is now used as a car park, while the current running lines are behind the fence on the left. *Jack Hodgkinson/TG*

NEATH GENERAL (2): On 27 September 1958 the 10.33am from Briton Ferry to Swansea is worked by 56XX No 6649, seen calling at Neath. This is a journey of only 10 miles and the train called at three of the four intermediate stations, omitting Landore High Level.

Neath is still a busy station and on 9 September 2000 up and down trains are seen passing. On the left is Class 158 No 158827 forming the 09.12 Pembroke Dock to Manchester Piccadilly service. The other train, headed by Class 43 No 43174, is the 09.00 from Paddington to Swansea. In the height of summer this train continued to Fishguard Harbour. *R. J. Buckley, courtesy Don Gatehouse/TG*

COURT SART: The GWR had a large locomotive depot at Court Sart, known as Neath and coded 87A in BR days. It closed in June 1965 and the land is now used as playing fields; all that remains is the footbridge over the main line that gave access to the depot. The depot and wagon repair shops to the right are seen on 22 September 1962, and the playing fields in March 2002. *Roger Carpenter/TG*

28XX Class No 3823 stands by the coaling stage at Court Sart on 31 April 1964. *Jack Hodgkinson*

COURT SART JUNCTION: An empty carriage working from Swansea behind 56XX Class No 5625 is seen at Court Sart Junction, between Neath and Briton Ferry, on 1 September 1961; it will form the return workman's train to Swansea. The lines to the left are goods only, while on the right under the bridge is the connecting line from the Swansea District Line (see page 90). The Rhondda & Swansea Bay Railway (RSBR) line also passed under this bridge, and its Court Sart station was to the right of the main-line signal box (see page 38). These lines were crossed by the South Wales Mineral Railway line to Tonmawr.

The 14.25 mail train from Swansea on 2 May 2001 is hauled by Class 67 No 67004. At Bristol vans from Plymouth are attached to this train, before it continues to London The lines to the left and right are still in use, but the line over the bridge was dismantled in 1910. *John Hodge, courtesy Don Gatehouse/TG*

BRITON FERRY (1): The GWR station is seen on 3 June 1963, looking towards Port Talbot. It was opened in 1935, combining the former GWR and RSBR stations on a new site (see opposite).

This station closed in November 1964 and a new station was built by BR 30 years later a few yards north, ie towards the camera. In May 2001 a First Great Western HST rushes through Briton Ferry forming the 14.30 Swansea to Paddington service. *P. J. Garland, courtesy Roger Carpenter/TG*

BRITON FERRY (2): The up 'Pembroke Coast Express' has just passed through Briton Ferry station (in the background) behind 'Castle' Class No 4094 *Dynevor Castle* on 27 June 1960. In the right foreground are the remains of the embankment of the RSBR, which also had a station here, latterly called Briton Ferry East; it closed in September 1935. Also to the right is the site of the GWR station known as Briton Ferry West. It closed in July 1935 with the opening of the new main-line station, which itself closed in 1964 (see opposite).

On 2 May 2001 Class 66 No 66137 passes the same point on a coal train from Cwmgwrach, which is on the GWR line along the Vale of Neath (see pages 77-80). *John Hodge, courtesy Don Gatehouse/TG*

BRITON FERRY (3): This is the GWR station of Briton Ferry West in 1953, 18 years after closure. The embankment and bridge abutments of the RSBR line are in the centre (see page 24), but these have since been removed and houses built on the levelled site. The GWR station has also been removed. *Adrian Vaughan/TG*

BRITON FERRY (4): Looking south towards Port Talbot from the main A483 road at Briton Ferry (the road to the left is the A48), the 4.55pm from Swansea to Cymmer Afan and Treherbert is seen from the rear taking the former RSBR line on 1 September 1961.

Much change has taken place to both the railways and the roads. A new bridge has been built over the railway and in the background is the M4 motorway, which also crosses the railway, while a footbridge has been built over the A48. No trace remains of the RSBR line to Cymmer Afan at this location. On 21 May 2000 the 16.30 Swansea to Paddington express passes the same point. *John Hodge, courtesy Don Gatehouse/TG*

PORT TALBOT GENERAL (1): The 4.45pm Sunday train from Porthcawl to Swansea High Street stops at Port Talbot General on 21 July 1957 headed by 51XX Class No 4107, then based at Landore Depot.

Port Talbot station was rebuilt in 1961 and is now an island platform. In September 2001 Class 43 No 43025 heads the 14.00 Paddington to Swansea service, which had been diverted via Gloucester due to engineering works in the Severn Tunnel. *Brian Morrison, courtesy Don Gatehouse/TG*

PORT TALBOT GENERAL (2): During rebuilding temporary buildings were erected on the up platform, at which the 12.40pm Carmarthen to Cheltenham train calls on 9 March 1961.

The terraced houses on the left have since been demolished and the station approach roads realigned. The major common landmark is a hotel, the tall building in the background. The station was renamed Port Talbot Parkway in 1984 to reflect its proximity to the M4 motorway. On 19 September 2001 Class 158 No 158746 forms the 11.50 Haverfordwest to Manchester Piccadilly service. *John Hodge, courtesy Don Gatehouse/TG*

PORT TALBOT GENERAL (3): Diesel locomotive No 1913 (later Class 47 No 47236) heads an up train at Port Talbot on 28 April 1973, while on 19 September 2001 the 13.30 Swansea to Paddington express leaves the station. A new road overbridge can just be seen in the background, which would give good views of the station except that it has unfriendly notices banning pedestrians, reinforced by video cameras. Stations beyond Port Talbot towards Cardiff are covered in *British Railways Past and Present No 28*. *F. Hornby/TG*

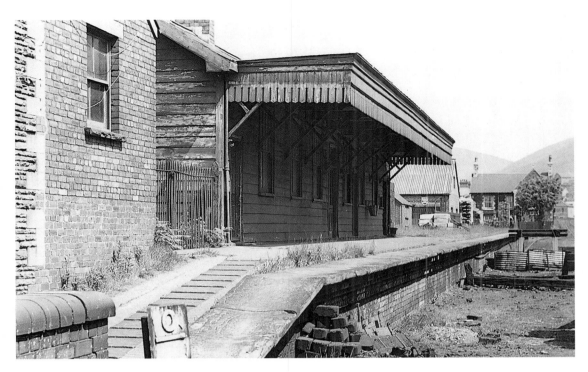

Port Talbot to Maesteg Neath Road

PORT TALBOT CENTRAL: The terminus of the Port Talbot Railway (PTR) was almost opposite the GWR main-line station, and after leaving the terminus the line skirted the rugby football ground, then headed up the valley to Maesteg. The line closed to passengers in September 1933, and Central is seen here in June 1953; although the track has been taken up in the station, the buffer stops mark the end of the line for freight trains, which continued until 1960.

Part of the site is now used for a telephone exchange and Royal Mail delivery office, and the remainder is occupied by houses. *N. L. Browne, courtesy F. Hornby/TG*

Opposite DUFFRYN YARD LOCO-MOTIVE DEPOT was a short distance from Port Talbot Central, and had an allocation of predominantly tank engines for local shunting and coal trains, as seen on 29 August 1948. No trace remains today, but the site is easily located from the adjacent hill. *Roger Carpenter/TG*

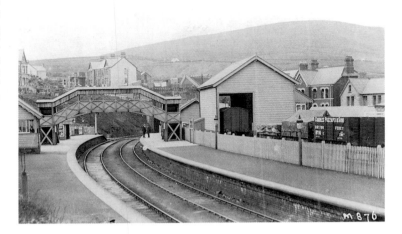

MAESTEG NEATH ROAD (1): The PTR station was in a cutting on the Neath Road on the western edge of the town, and these three photographs were taken in 1908, 1959 and 2001. The station lost its passenger service in 1933, but the line remained in use for freight until 1964. *Courtesy Robin Simmonds/ R. M. Casserley/TG*

MAESTEG NEATH ROAD (2): The PTR line continued to curve to the right beyond the bridge under Neath Road, then passed over the GWR line from Bridgend. The 'past' photograph, looking west, was taken on 14 July 1959.

A visit in September 2001 found the track of the GWR line still in place, although out of use. Passenger trains still run up the valley as far as a new Maesteg station in the town centre (see *British Railways Past and Present No 28*). *H. C. Casserley/TG*

Swansea Riverside to Aberavon and Blaengwynfi

SWANSEA RIVERSIDE (1): The Rhondda & Swansea Bay Railway (RSBR) had its Swansea terminus in the dock area very close to the GWR's East Dock station and the Midland Railway's St Thomas station. Originally called Swansea, then Swansea Docks, it was renamed Riverside in 1926. It closed to passengers in 1933, having closed to goods traffic in 1922. The April 1953 photograph shows the track still in place, while a visit in May 2000 found one of the platforms and an adjacent building still in existence. *R. Griffiths/TG*

SWANSEA RIVERSIDE (2): There was an extensive network of lines around the docks, and here we see former Swansea Harbour Trust (SHT) engine, GWR No 1140 of Danygraig Shed, passing through the streets of Swansea on its way to the docks in 1954.

The track has since been removed from the streets, but the imposing building of Swansea Museum on the right still stands in 2000. *Alan Jarvis/TG*

DANYGRAIG LOCOMOTIVE DEPOT: The RSBR line ran parallel with the GWR line and in less than a mile from the terminus was Danygraig locomotive depot, which housed many small tank engines for shunting in the docks. On 7 June 1953 the depot displayed (from left to right) engines Nos 8720 (57XX Class), 1142 (ex-SHT), 1104 (1101 Class) and 1143 (ex-SHT) facing the camera.

The depot closed in 1964 and is currently used by a chemical company, while the line in the right foreground serves the nearby Ford motor factory. Access is from Swansea Burrows Yard, which is behind the camera; the line into Swansea Burrows is beyond the far left side of Danygraig depot. *N. L. Browne, courtesy F. Hornby/TG*

COURT SART: The RSBR line crossed the Afon Nedd, then went under the GWR main line between Neath and Briton Ferry to a station at Court Sart, and the 'past' photograph shows the remains of this station in 1957.

A visit in 2000 found that the station had gone and the building on the left was being used by a car repairer. In the background the roofs of the houses of Morgan Terrace are visible. *Adrian Vaughan/TG*

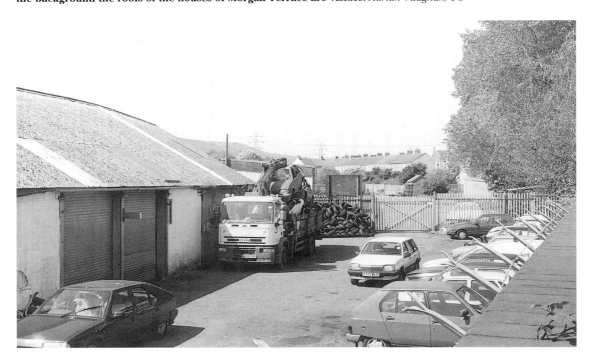

NEATH CANAL SIDE: The RSBR had its own station at Neath, a terminus known as Canal Bridge from 1924 and Canal Side two years later. A frequent shuttle service was run to and from Court Sart until the line closed to passengers in 1935, but it remained open for goods and the rare visits of special passenger trains, as seen here in 1956, until closure in September 1965.

The branch is now dissected by a new main road that passes on an embankment in front of the gasholder, which still exists. The station itself has gone and the land used by industrial units. The canal is immediately behind the hedge on the right. *R. M. Casserley/TG*

PORT TALBOT DOCKS (RSBR): The RSBR line ran parallel to the GWR main line past Briton Ferry (see page 24) to its own station of Briton Ferry East (see page 25). It then passed under the GWR main line, still running parallel to the main line; this section closed in 1962 and is under the A4241 road. At Port Talbot the RSBR had a station in the Docks, but this closed to passengers in 1895 when the company extended its line to Swansea, although it remained open for freight. Port Talbot Docks signal box was still in existence in 1952, but by 2001 it was difficult to locate the station site, and the best estimate is shown in the bottom photograph. *Adrian Vaughan/TG*

ABERAVON TOWN: Immediately north of Port Talbot's GWR station the RSBR line crossed the main line to a station called Aberavon Town, where a train of coal empties hauled by 57XX Class No 9799 is seen on 22 May 1958.

This is another difficult site to locate as a new shopping area has been built and few old buildings remain, although the large building on the opposite side of the river serves as a landmark, being just beyond the level crossing in the 'past' photograph. The filling station sign states 'Help Reduce Air Pollution' – try travelling by train! *Hugh Davies/TG*

CYMMER (1): The line followed the Afon Afan to Cymmer where there were large yards, mostly for coal traffic. Cymmer had three stations, belonging to the RSBR (Cymmer Afan), GWR (Cymmer General) and SWMR (Cymmer Corrwg). The RSBR and GWR stations were adjacent, and this is the GWR station, which from the 1960s until closure was used by trains to both Bridgend (the GWR line) and Swansea (the RSBR line); the refreshment rooms at the RSBR station are on the extreme right. An Abergwynfi to Bridgend service is worked by 45XX Class No 5545 in the 1960s. The trestle bridge in the distance carries the connecting line between the GWR line from Bridgend and Maesteg Castle Street to the SWMR to Glyncorrwg. *R. O. Tuck, courtesy Don Gatehouse/TG*

CYMMER (2): The two stations side by side are seen more clearly in this 1958 view up the valley. The GWR's general station is on the right and the RSBR's Cymmer Afan to the left. The latter's remaining station building still serves as a refreshment room, as seen in 2001. *Adrian Vaughan/TG*

CYMMER (3): Looking west in 1964, this view shows the replacement signal box and the Bridgend line curving off to the left. After closure, the signal box and lever frame were relocated to Bargoed in the Rhymney Valley, and both are still in use in 2001. The 'present' photograph illustrates the dramatic changes that can take place on the mountainsides of South Wales. *Adrian Vaughan/TG*

CYMMER (4): The last views of Cymmer show a passenger train behind 51XX Class No 4121 on 13 June 1960, and at the present day, where part of the site is occupied by a tennis court. *David Lawrence, courtesy Hugh Davies/TG*

45

BLAENGWYNFI (1) was the next station up the valley on the RSBR line, where a train waits to leave for Bridgend behind 57XX Class No 9609 on 15 October 1960.

The line closed in June 1970, and a visit in 1993 found the station gone and housing and a new road in its place. However, the course of the railway is still apparent in the background. *E. T. Gill/Don Gatehouse*

BLAENGWYNFI (2): This more distant view of Blaengwynfi in 1960 shows that north-east of the station was the Rhondda Tunnel, which was closed to all traffic in 1968 because of instability. In the foreground is the GWR line to Abergwynfi. The second photograph is the same view in 1993. *R. O. Tuck/Geoff Dowling, both courtesy Don Gatehouse*

ABERGWYNFI: Looking towards the buffer stops at the GWR terminus of Abergwynfi on 29 August 1951, the first member of the 31XX Class, No 3100, is signalled to leave for Bridgend. The line to the right was for freight only and continued a further half-mile to Avon Colliery. The tall building to the left of the station is the Great Western Hotel.

Passenger services were withdrawn in June 1960, and a visit in 1993 found the station site cleared, but the hotel building still in use and now simply called 'Great Western'. *Ian L. Wright, courtesy Don Gatehouse/Don Gatehouse*

49

Cymmer Corrwg to North Rhondda

GLYNCORRWG (1): The third station at Cymmer, on the South Wales Mineral Railway (SWMR), was on the other side of the valley from the GWR and RSBR stations and was a single platform. The line ran along the western bank of the Afon Corrwg to the village of Glyncorrwg, which could also be reached by a parallel road on the other bank of the river. There is an excellent view of the railway at Glyncorrwg from the adjacent hillside, and looking up the valley towards North Rhondda on 2 June 1960 we see a special train propelled by 57XX Class No 9634. It is apparent from the April 2001 view that many of the surrounding buildings still exist, including the corrugated building in the former station yard. *R. J. Buckley, courtesy Don Gatehouse/TG*

GLYNCORRWG (2): Looking down the valley toward Cymmer about 1950 from the level crossing at Glyncorrwg, a miners' train is seen, with the engine at one end and the driver, travelling in the end compartment of the leading coach, at the other; such an 'auto-train' arrangement was used as there was insufficient space to run round the train at the head of the valley.

In contrast to many of the other locations visited in the course of preparing this book, on this line the trackbed has not been obscured by redevelopment or nature, other than at the two ends. The building with the high windows on the right is the community centre, while the aforementioned surviving corrugated hut can be seen on the left. *R. W. A. Jones, courtesy Don Gatehouse/TG*

NORTH RHONDDA (1): The line continued a short distance up the valley to the collieries at North Rhondda, where a simple wooden platform was provided. This is a 1950s view, looking down the valley to Glyncorrwg.
The river has been diverted as part of land reclamation, but as best as can be judged the 'present' view is the same location today. *R. W. A. Jones, courtesy Don Gatehouse/TG*

NORTH RHONDDA (2): The miners' train, behind engine No 9634, is seen in about 1950, looking up the valley. The miners' service ceased in 1961, and the line was abandoned when the mines closed.

Since the closure an unbelievable transformation has taken place through a huge reclamation scheme. The result is that the area is unrecognisable and the author spent some long time looking for clues to identify exactly the same viewpoints. These two photographs, taken on the same day in 2001 and also looking up the valley, give an indication of the extent of the change. The only identifiable feature is a remnant of the stone retaining wall of the railway embankment.

R. W. A. Jones, courtesy Don Gatehouse/TG (2)

Neath towards Brecon

NEATH RIVERSIDE (1): The Neath & Brecon Railway (NBR) station at Neath was crossed by Bridge Street, after which it was named shortly after the Grouping of the main railway companies in 1923, then in 1926 it was renamed Riverside. In the station on 9 May 1953 is 57XX Class No 3611 on a train to Onllwyn and Brecon.

The second view, taken on 18 May 1958, shows that the platforms have lost their awnings and the footbridge has been removed. Immediately behind the camera is the overbridge carrying the main GWR line from Swansea to London.

The station lost its regular passenger service in 1962, but a slightly more restricted view was obtained from a special passenger train hauled by Class 66 No 66145 on 16 March 2002. In the background is a new public footbridge over the railway. *John Edgington, courtesy Don Gatehouse/Norman Simmons, courtesy Hugh Davies/TG*

NEATH RIVERSIDE (2): The view from Bridge Street (now pedestrian only) at the other end of the station enabled trains to be observed on both the NBR and GWR lines. On 18 May 1958 an up train crosses the NBR line en route to Neath General (GWR) station and beyond.

In September 2000 a coal train from Onllwyn passes through Riverside station on its way to Swansea Burrows, where the engine, Class 66 No 66055, will run round and the train will continue through Briton Ferry to Aberthaw power station. The signal box is still in use. *Norman Simmons, courtesy Hugh Davies/TG*

NEATH (NBR) LOCOMOTIVE SHED was the other side of the GWR main line bridge and adjacent to the line to Brecon. On 4 May 1952 several 57XX Class pannier tanks are on shed.

The shed closed in 1964, but it was not until 2000 that the site was redeveloped, and is now occupied by houses, which were still being built at the time of a visit in September of that year. The line on the extreme right is used by the coal trains to and from Onllwyn. *Norman Simmons, courtesy Hugh Davies/TG*

This photograph, taken on 1 May 2001 in very poor evening light, shows the Onllwyn line in the foreground and a train from Cwmgwrach (Vale of Neath line, see pages 77-80) on the right, headed by Class 66 No 66146. The vandal-proof 'garage' in the centre is for the signalman's car. *TG*

PENSCYNOR HALT: There were several halts on the line up the valley, the second of which was Penscynor, 1½ miles from Neath Riverside. Waiting passengers are seen from the train window as a Brecon train approaches the halt on 27 September 1958. The St John's Ambulance Hall acted as a landmark for a visit in May 2001. *R. J. Buckley, courtesy Don Gatehouse/TG*

CEFN COED COLLIERY HALT was the next stop, opened in 1930 for the adjacent colliery. The Winter 1961/62 timetable shows that only public trains travelling down the valley stopped here. The colliery was rail connected and this early 1900s photograph shows the extent of coal traffic.

Today the extensive yards have gone and the colliery is closed. In its place, using several of the original buildings, is an excellent colliery museum. *Courtesy National Museums & Galleries of Wales Department of Industry/TG*

BLAENANT COLLIERY: In more recent times coal trains were worked by Class 37s. This train, hauled by No 37270 and a sister engine, is at Blaenant Colliery, which was built on the same site as Cefn Coed. Blaenant closed in May 1990.

The 'present' photograph shows the location in March 2002. Coal trains now pass through Cefn Coed on a regular basis to a washery at Onllwyn. Cefn Coed Colliery Halt was situated just out of sight round the corner.
Cefn Coed Colliery Museum/TG

CRYNANT (1) is three-quarters of a mile further up the valley, and had a station with a passing loop. A coal train heads down the valley on 24 February 1962.

The loop has been removed and only remnants of the platforms remain. The view of the mountains is now very restricted. *C. J. Gammell/TG*

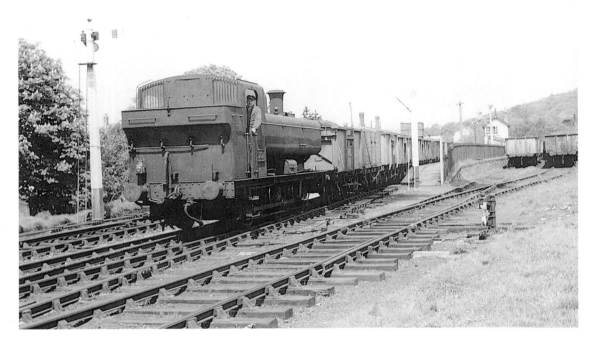

CRYNANT (2): Another down coal train, hauled by 57XX Class No 7757, passes through Crynant in May 1958. A residential development now occupies the site of the yard, and the houses can be seen on the extreme right in the 2001 photograph. *Norman Simmons, courtesy Hugh Davies/TG*

SEVEN SISTERS (1): A train for Brecon stops at Seven Sisters on 5 May 1960. All that remains today is the iron footbridge, which is still in use, although there is talk of removing it because of vandalism. *E. T. Gill, courtesy Hugh Davies/TG*

SEVEN SISTERS (2): By the time of a visit in February 1962 the platform awning had been removed, and the station closed in October of the same year. The overbridge carries the road from Neath to Colbren. An extended wait for a coal train on 30 April 2001 resulted in disappointment. *C. J. Gammell/TG*

PANTYFFORDD HALT stood beside the Neath to Colbren road to serve the community of Pantyffordd, three-quarters of a mile beyond Seven Sisters. On 14 July 1960 57XX Class No 4627 is working the 4.10pm train from Neath Riverside to Brecon, stopping at all stations and halts except Cefn Coed.

On 30 April 2001 the long-awaited coal train suddenly appeared, hauled by Class 66 No 66094; in the days of trains double-headed by Class 37s, there would have been ample warning of an approaching train. Only a mound of earth and the stem of the milepost are left as reminders of the halt. *S. C. L. Phillips/TG*

ONLLWYN station served the village and colliery of the same name, and this is the view looking down the valley from the road bridge by the station on 12 June 1962. The colliery is situated behind the camera.

A broader view from the same bridge was taken on 2 May 2001, when Class 66 No 66043 was engaged in shunting. Until recent times the signal box had been used as a chargeman's office, but was demolished in 2002.
Adrian Vaughan/TG

ONLLWYN COLLIERY (1): The colliery sidings are seen from the road by the station on 28 March 1959; on the extreme left is the line to Colbren Junction.

Even today Onllwyn is an interesting place to observe coal trains. There are usually two per day, both of which spend typically 2-3 hours in the sidings. The present-day photograph was taken from the same road, but nearer to the station; the remains of the line to Colbren Junction can clearly be seen. The corrugated-roofed building in the 'past' photograph still exists, but is just out of view on the extreme right. *Michael Hale/TG*

ONLLWYN COLLIERY (2): The first, pre-1900, photograph of the colliery and station shows that the Half Way Inn has yet to be built to the left of the station; in the second photograph it is just being completed, as seen in the centre background.

The third undated photograph, probably from the early part of the 20th century, shows a busy railway yard. The present-day view reveals that the inn has been demolished, but the railway yard is still used. *Courtesy National Museums & Galleries of Wales Department of Industry (3)/TG*

COLBREN JUNCTION (1) is seen on 14 July 1960 with the 6.20pm Brecon to Neath train ready to depart behind 57XX Class No 3714. The trees help to identify the location today. *Hugh Ballantyne, courtesy Don Gatehouse/TG*

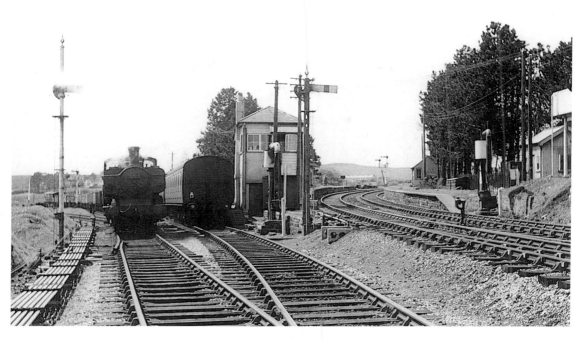

COLBREN JUNCTION (2): When viewed from the other direction, the two lines constituting the junction can be seen. To the left is the Neath line and to the right the line to Ynys-y-Geinon Junction and the Midland Railway route to Swansea St Thomas. On 20 May 1958 a train of coal empties has just come up the valley and a passenger train waits to leave for Neath. The section between Colbren Junction and Ynys-y-Geinon closed to passengers in 1932. *Norman Simmons, courtesy Hugh Davies/TG*

CRAIG-Y-NOS: Just north of Colbren the railway entered what is now the Brecon Beacons National Park. The isolated nature of Craig-y-Nos station is captured in this photograph taken on 14 July 1960 as a train bound for Neath departs.

The station building still exists and in the intervening years offices have been erected for the adjacent quarry. Freight ceased to run from Onllwyn northward in 1963, but was re-instated as far as Craig-y-Nos the following year for the quarry. It was out of use again by 1977, and closed officially in 1981. For the line on towards Brecon, see *British Railways Past and Present No 32*. *S. C. L. Phillips, courtesy Don Gatehouse/TG*

Swansea East Dock to Glyn Neath

SWANSEA EAST DOCK station is seen here in 1930, six years before closure to passenger services, although it remained open for freight until the 1980s. It was also used for berthing locomotives, and several Class 37s (the front two being Nos 6600 and 6978) are seen there on 28 April 1973. All track and buildings have since been cleared and the site is derelict, the only common attribute being the church spire in the background. *Courtesy R. G. Simmonds/F. Hornby/ TG*

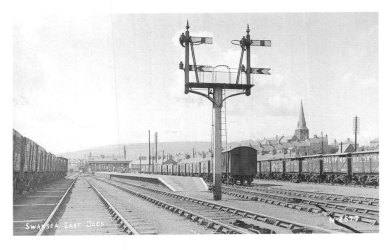

SWANSEA EAST DOCK LOCOMOTIVE DEPOT was a short distance to the east, and is seen here with a 'crowd' of pannier tanks in 1958. The shed floor and part of the coaling stage ramp are all that is left in 2001. *H. R. Newey, courtesy D. K. Jones/TG*

ABERDYLAIS HALT: The GWR line from East Dock ran parallel to the RSBR line almost to Neath. In the 1890s trains ran only between East Dock and Neath Low Level (ie Bridge Street, later Riverside), but a service was later introduced up the Vale of Neath (Cwm Nedd) to Pontypool Road. Just north of Neath was Aberdylais Halt, seen from a train heading for Pontypool Road in 1964. After closure of Swansea East Dock station, trains ran from Swansea High Street to Neath General, where they reversed to gain access to the line between Bridge Street and Aberdylais Halt.

The line is still used almost to Glyn Neath and on 1 May 2001 Class 66 No 66146 passes the old platform on an empty stone train up the valley. This train was due *down* the valley at this time on its return journey, and was running about 6½ hours late (see page 59). *Jack Hodgkinson/TG*

RESOLVEN is seen here looking up the valley on a wet day in the summer of 1956, while the 'present' photograph shows the station in May 2001. Part of the platforms still exist, as do the terraced houses on the left, but new houses have been built on the right-hand side. *R. M. Casserley/TG*

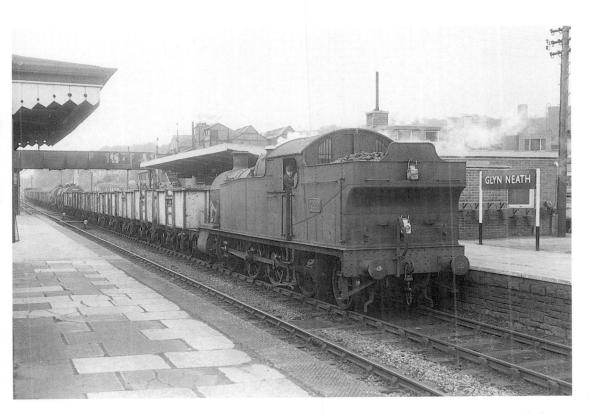

GLYN NEATH was a busy railway centre with station, engine shed and extensive yards to serve the coal industry. On 3 April 1964 a coal train headed by 72XX Class No 7222 passes through the station on its way down the valley.

Nothing whatever is left of Glyn Neath today, the station site being partly under new roads and the rest of the land derelict. *Jack Hodgkinson/TG*

GLYN NEATH LOCOMOTIVE DEPOT was adjacent to the station, and on 12 May 1956 42XX Class No 4252 is under the water tower.

A new main road now passes through the site, on the edge of which is a McDonald's fast food restaurant. The present line terminates just before this point at Cwmgwrach, which handles coal and aggregates. For stations on towards Pontypool Road see *British Railways Past and Present Nos 26 and 28*. *W. Potter, courtesy Don Gatehouse/TG*

(70)   Rhymney Railway.

Glyn Neath

G.W.R.

Swansea St Thomas to Brynamman East

SWANSEA ST THOMAS was the Midland Railway's terminus, close to the Riverside station of the RSBR. Class 3F No 47479 takes a single-coach train to Ystalyfera on 2 September 1950, three weeks before closure.

The station lay abandoned for many years, and the second photograph was taken prior to 1965, when the Bridge Inn was demolished.

The site is now a public park and surrounding road improvements have also resulted in demolition of the houses to the left of the station. *Ian L. Wright, courtesy Don Gatehouse/David Lawrence, courtesy Hugh Davies/TG*

UPPER BANK was the next station, only 1½ miles from the terminus; the former Midland Railway signal box is prominent on the left. This was the junction for lines via Morriston East (foreground) or Llansamlet South (left), which met again at Glais Junction, and this was the view looking towards Swansea on 30 June 1957.

A goods service was retained until 1964, and the now derelict site was visited on 29 April 2001. *R. J. Buckley, courtesy Don Gatehouse/TG*

UPPER BANK LOCOMOTIVE DEPOT was a small facility and a subshed of Swansea Victoria. It closed in 1963 and has since been demolished.

However, there is new life here, as Upper Bank is the headquarters of the Swansea Vale Railway, which uses a former foundry as its workshop. In the background is the same long building that is seen on the extreme right of the 'past' photograph. The running lines are on the far left. *H. R. Newey, courtesy D. K. Jones/TG*

CLYDACH-ON-TAWE: There was a station at Morriston (East), close to the GWR station (see page 89), followed by Clydach-on-Tawe, seen here on 15 September 1962. The station was in an industrial area, and this remains true today, with many of the old industrial buildings still in use. *C. J. Gammell/TG*

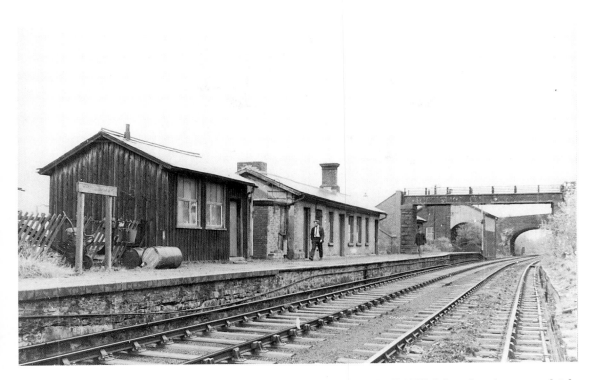

PONTARDAWE was another uninspiring station, photographed on 24 April 1965. It has since been completely obliterated and the site is now under a new main road. The location was deduced from a nearby river bridge and the road that used to cross the railway. *J. M. Tolson, courtesy F. Hornby/TG*

BRYNAMMAN EAST: At Ynys-y-Geinon Junction the line forked to Colbren (see pages 72 and 73) and Brynamman East (the suffix East was added in 1950). This is the station on 9 August 1958, showing the small terminal platform, behind which is an 'Odeon'-style cinema. On the right is the connecting line to Brynamman West, which was not used by passenger trains (see page 124).

The site is currently used as the living quarters and equipment storage for a fairground family. The 'Odeon' still stands. *C. J. Gammell/TG*

Swansea High Street to Morriston West

NEAR MORRISTON WEST: This was a GWR local line that ran through Landore (Low Level) to Copper Pit and Morriston West. On 18 May 1958 main-line trains were diverted on to this line, and the 12.25pm Milford Haven to Paddington, behind 'Castle' Class No 5041 *Tiverton Castle*, is seen between Copper Pit and Morriston.

The line closed to passengers in June 1956 and completely in 1965, and a new main road has been built over much of its length, but remnants of the stone retaining wall on this section still exist. The footbridge on the left crosses the new main road. *Norman Simmons, courtesy Hugh Davies/TG*

SWANSEA DISTRICT LINE: From Morriston the line was extended in May 1914 to connect with the Swansea District Line, which had just been built. The purpose of the District Line was to allow trains to avoid the congested lines around Swansea and the steep gradients at Cockett (see pages 91-2). The newly built line, which ran from Llanelly (Llandilo Junction), is seen from a point about halfway between the junctions with the Morriston and main GWR lines (Felin Fran Junction and Skewen Junction East respectively). The railway passing under the District Line is the Midland Railway line from Upper Bank to Glais Junction via Llansamlet South (see page 83).

A visit in April 2001 found that, apart from the introduction of electricity pylons and the usual encroachment of vegetation, little had changed. Very few trains currently use this line. *Courtesy R. G. Simmonds/TG*

Swansea High Street towards Llanelly

COCKETT TUNNEL (1): The GWR main line from Swansea High Street takes the south side of the triangle at Landore (see pages 15-18), then heads west through Cockett Tunnel. 'Hall' Class No 4981 *Abberley Hall* climbs Cockett Bank with a Paddington to Fishguard train in the summer of 1961.

On 20 May 2000 a Wales & West train, the 12.11 Swansea to Tenby consisting of Class 153 Nos 153370 and 153382, makes light work of the climb. At the west end of the tunnel is the remains of Cockett station, which closed in 1964. A little beyond here the line has been singled. *Andrew F. Smith, courtesy Don Gatehouse/TG*

COCKETT TUNNEL (2): 'Hall' Class No 5937 *Stanford Hall* emerges from Cockett Tunnel with the 12.05pm Milford Haven to Paddington on 21 June 1961. The inclusion of vacuum-fitted vans for fish, parcels, etc, was commonplace even on prestigious express passenger trains.

On 20 May 2000 the single coach of Class 153 No 153374 forms the 08.55 from Shrewsbury to Swansea. *Andrew F. Smith, courtesy Don Gatehouse/TG*

GOWERTON NORTH (GWR) (1): There were two stations at Gowerton, the GWR facility being named Gowerton North from the beginning of 1950, reverting to plain Gowerton in May 1968. In this photograph of the goods yard and main line on 5 June 1963, the station can be seen in the background.

The yard is now closed, part being occupied by small industrial units and the remainder abandoned. The main line lies to the right, out of sight. *Adrian Vaughan/TG*

GOWERTON NORTH (GWR) (2): Looking from the end of the platform back towards the goods yard in May 1958, we see 'Castle' Class No 7002 *Devizes Castle* on the 11.55am Paddington to Pembroke Dock train.

The same month 42 years later sees Class 153 No 153370 making a stop by request as the 13.23 Swansea to Shrewsbury service. *N. C. Simmons, courtesy Hugh Davies/TG*

LOUGHOR station was located by the river of the same name. A DMU enters the station on a train bound for Swansea in the early 1960s.

The line has since been singled, the station closed and demolished, and the road upgraded, all of which has made the view far less attractive. *Adrian Vaughan/TG*

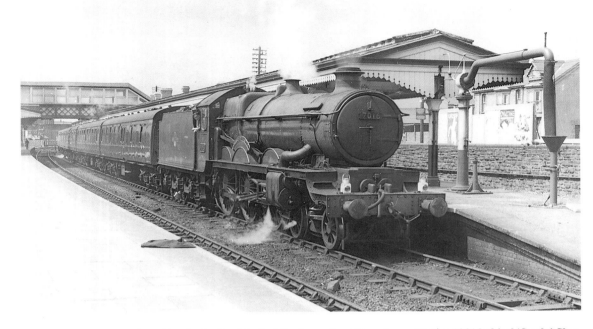

LLANELLY: An express from Pembroke Dock to Paddington calls at Llanelly on 26 May 1961 behind 'Castle' Class No 7016 *Chester Castle.*
    From Summer 2002 all trains are operated by Wales & Borders on Mondays to Fridays, except for one First Great Western train in each direction. On 20 May 2000 single-coach Class 153 unit No 153327 forms the 10.05 from Swansea to Pembroke Dock. *P. Hutchinson/TG*

LLANELLY LOCOMOTIVE DEPOT: There was a large motive power depot at Llanelly, the extent of which is seen in this photograph taken on 21 September 1962. The area has since been flattened and the site can only be identified by reference to surrounding streets. The lines west of Llanelly are covered in *British Railways Past and Present No 38*. *R. S. Carpenter/TG*

Swansea Victoria to Llandilo (including the Llanmorlais branch)

Other photographs of this line are to be found in *Past and Present Companion: The Central Wales Line* – see the Bibliography.

SWANSEA VICTORIA was the LNWR's station in Swansea, and was certainly more imposing than that of the Midland Railway. On 29 June 1949 the Pontardulais train is worked appropriately by an ex-LNWR engine, Class 2F No 27625. The shedplate 4B is Swansea, which later became 87K under the Western Region. On the right is Class 4MT No 42390. The station roof was damaged by bombing during the Second World War and was never repaired.

The line was transferred to the Western Region the same year, and inevitably pannier tanks took over the passenger trains. The second photograph shows 74XX Class No 7408 on 9 August 1958.

The line lost its passenger service in 1964 and closed completely the following year. The station has now gone and the land redeveloped to include a leisure centre. *Ian L. Wright, courtesy Don Gatehouse/C. J. Gammell/TG*

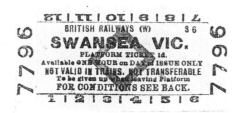

SWANSEA BAY: The line ran alongside the Swansea & Mumbles Railway and followed the coast through Swansea Bay station, seen here on 11 June 1960. Class 5MT No 45143 brings the 9.50pm train from York towards Victoria, where it is due to arrive at 8.18am.

The area has since been cleared, but the major landmark of the stadium on the right helps to locate the site of the station. *Hugh Ballantyne/TG*

MUMBLES ROAD was where the line swung inland, and the neatly turned out station is seen in August 1958. A park now occupies the site, and the trackbed has become 'The Swansea Bike Path'. *C. J. Gammell/TG*

KILLAY was another pleasant station, seen here on 16 June 1963. Today the yard has become a collection point for the recycling of domestic waste, but the station building survives and is just visible through the trees (and the rain!) on the extreme left. *C. J. Gammell/TG*

DUNVANT was in a cutting on the east side of the village. Immediately behind the camera is a road overbridge, which no longer affords a high vantage point as trees block the view. The photographs were taken in June 1963 and May 2000. The platform is in the foreground. *C. J. Gammell/TG*

GOWERTON SOUTH (LNWR): Class 3F No 47481 is seen at Gowerton South on the 4.05pm train from Swansea Victoria to Pontardulais on 19 May 1958. Today the site has been made most attractive by conversion to a small park. *Norman Simmons courtesy Hugh Davies/TG*

PENCLAWDD: Gowerton South was the junction for the Llanmorlais branch, the only intermediate station being at Penclawdd. A visit on 16 June 1963 found that the track had been lifted following complete closure in September 1957, while a visit in the spring of 2000 found the platform still in existence and the station and adjacent houses tastefully renovated. *C. J. Gammell/TG*

LLANMORLAIS: Class 3F No 47480 arrives at Llanmorlais on a railtour on 2 July 1955, 24 years after the cessation of regular passenger trains. By 1963 the track had been removed, and in 2000 there was little trace of the terminus. *Ian L. Wright, courtesy Don Gatehouse/C. J. Gammell/TG*

GORSEINON: Back on the LNWR main line, the first station north of Gowerton was Gorseinon, built in the same style as the stations nearer Swansea. The June 1963 view shows the main Llanelly to Neath road crossing the railway.

A visit in 2000 found that the station site has been used for a new road, and nothing remains of the railway.
C. J. Gammell/TG

PONTARDULAIS was where the LNWR line was joined by the GWR line from Llanelly, the latter on the right of this August 1958 photograph. The view is dominated by the lengthy standard-pattern GWR footbridge, which extends over sidings to the left.

The LNWR line closed completely in June 1964 and all that is left is a gap in the trees. Pontardulais now has just one platform, used by the Swansea to Shrewsbury trains on the Central Wales Line, which reverse at Llanelly.
C. J. Gammell/TG

LLANGENNECH: On the GWR line going south from Pontardulais, there were two intermediate stations before the junction with the GWR main line (Llandilo Junction) just east of Llanelly. The first is Llangennech, and on 26 May 1956 up and down trains have just crossed. This section of the line (below Morlais South Junction) is also the westerly end of the Swansea District line (see page 90).

On 20 May 2000 Class 153 No 153327 passes through the request-only station forming the 05.25 Crewe to Swansea High Street service. *N. L. Browne, courtesy F. Hornby/TG*

BYNEA is the second station, and this is the view looking toward Llanelly on 5 June 1963 and 20 May 2000; note the centre-balanced signals in the 'past' photograph. In the 'present' view, the train consists of Class 153 No 153305 operating the 08.08 Cardiff Central to Shrewsbury service. *Adrian Vaughan/TG*

PANTYFFYNNON is the first station north of Pontardulais, and is another junction station. On 15 June 1963 Class 4MT No 80069 leaves the station with a southbound Central Wales train. To the right is the branch for Brynamman West, which lost its passenger service in 1958. On 19 May 2000 the Central Wales train consists of a single-coach unit of Class 153, No 153380, forming the 08.55 service from Shrewsbury. The Brynamman West branch still exists as far as Garnant (see page 125), and was used for the conveyance of coal from Gwaun-cae-Gurwen until 1999; it is currently mothballed.
C. J. Gammell/TG

113

AMMANFORD & TIRYDAIL is the next station on the Central Wales line. Formerly named just Tirydail, it became Ammanford & Tirydail, then simply Ammanford when the Brynamman branch station of that name closed. It was a single-platform station with a passing goods loop, as seen on 15 June 1963.

The loop was later taken out and the station building removed, but all trains (other than specials) make a mandatory stop here. *C. J. Gammell/TG*

LLANDEBIE is seen on 15 June 1963 and 9 September 2000, the latter with Class 153 No 153374 forming the 05.25 service from Crewe to Swansea High Street, which the author had boarded at Shrewsbury. *C. J. Gammell/TG*

DERWYDD ROAD: Class 5MT No 73056 enters the abandoned station on 19 May 1964 with the 6.25am Swansea Victoria to York train. Derwydd Road had closed 10 years previously and Swansea Victoria was to close a month later. The signal box and passing loop were still functional and the signalman stands ready to exchange the single-line tokens. The base of the signal box and remnants of the platforms were found during a May 2000 visit.
Hugh Ballantyne/TG

FFAIRFACH had become unstaffed in 1961, and is seen here in June 1963, by which time it was shown in public timetables as Ffairfach Halt, and at which few trains stopped.

It is currently served by all trains on a request basis, and several passengers joined the train at the time of the author's visit in May 2000. *C. J. Gammell/TG*

LLANDILO (1): As indicated on the station nameboard, Llandilo was the junction for the LNWR line to Carmarthen (see *British Railways Past and Present No 38*). This is Llandilo on 16 June 1963, looking towards Shrewsbury.

On 19 May 2000 Class 153 No 153302 arrives forming the 08.22 service from Bridgend to Shrewsbury. The station is devoid of most of the old buildings and the bay, but still has a passing loop. *C. J. Gammell/TG*

LLANDILO (2): A northbound train on the Central Wales line enters Llandilo behind Class 5MT No 45422 in May 1958. In the foreground is 74XX Class pannier tank No 7425 on a Carmarthen train.

By contrast, in May 2000 Class 153 No 153302 approaches the station. The stations further north are covered in *Past and Present Companion: The Central Wales Line*. *Norman Simmons, courtesy Hugh Davies/TG*

Pantyffynnon to Garnant, Brynamman West and Gwaun-cae-Gurwen

AMMANFORD was the first station on the branch, not to be confused with the present-day Ammanford half a mile away on the Central Wales line (see page 114). The first photograph shows the station on 19 May 1958, three months prior to closure.

The station site in May 2001 shows traces of the platforms and a trackbed free of both weeds and rubbish. There are no scheduled trains on this line. *Norman Simmons, courtesy Hugh Davies/TG*

AMMANFORD COLLIERY HALT was a little further along the branch, photographed on the same two days. In 1958 Ammanford Colliery Sidings signal box can be seen, which controlled access to the colliery, situated some distance away to the right across the River Amman. The old entrance to the halt from the nearby road can still be seen. *Norman Simmons, courtesy Hugh Davies/TG*

GLANAMMAN is seen shortly before closure in August 1958, with a train heading up the valley behind 57XX Class No 9743. At first glance there is little difference between the 1958 and 2001 photographs – both track and signal box are still there, but there is no platform surface. The line could be opened to passengers again, and indeed there is such a proposal in conjunction with the development of a country park at Gwaun-cae-Gurwen. *C. J. Gammell/TG*

GARNANT (1): Another photograph of No 9743 in August 1958, this time at Garnant in the Brynamman West platform. Garnant was a junction station and the platform for Gwaun-cae-Gurwen is on the left where the building can be seen beyond the locomotive (see page 125).

On 30 April 2001 it was very difficult to find this exact location. Much of the station area is now a park and the nearby roads have been widened and realigned, despite the fact that the line to Gwaun-cae-Gurwen is still in place. The iron railings and the other platform, out of sight beyond, give the clues. *C. J. Gammell/TG*

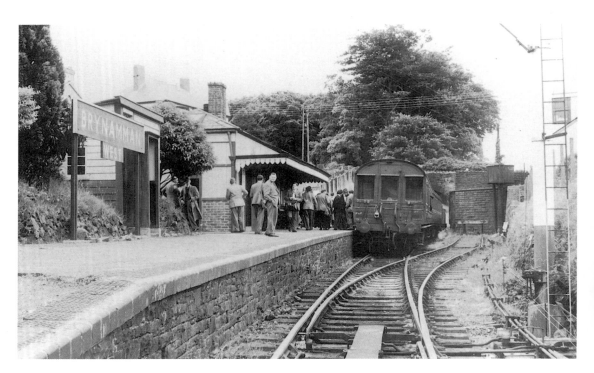

BRYNAMMAN WEST: This is the terminus for passenger trains at Brynamman West, showing a special train on 2 July 1955. The line continues under the road bridge to Brynamman East (see page 88).

The cutting is now filled in, but the house (upper left) is still in existence, as seen in the photograph of the station site on 19 May 2000. *R. J. Buckley, courtesy Don Gatehouse/TG*

GARNANT (2): Returning to Garnant, this is the platform for Gwaun-cae-Gurwen, in which stand 57XX Class No 7718 and a brake-van on 19 May 1958.

A visit on 19 May 2000 found both the platform and one of the buildings (behind the trees on the left). During a visit a year later a railway contractor's van drew up and the occupants, after donning high-visibility vests, proceeded to paint the level crossing fencing, on a line that has not had a regular passenger or freight train for **years.** *N. C. Simmons, courtesy Hugh Davies/TG*

GWAUN-CAE-GURWEN (1): The same engine and brake-van are seen again, this time crossing the road at Gwaun-cae-Gurwen. Beyond the crossing were sidings for coal wagons from the nearby collieries.

A May 2001 visit found that the footbridge had been removed, but the track was in good order and new traditional level crossing gates had been fitted. The shop on the extreme right is still open. *N. C. Simmons, courtesy Hugh Davies/TG*

GWAUN-CAE-GURWEN (2): The GWR had plans to extend the line south and connect it to its freight-only line at Clydach-on-Tawe and thence to the Swansea District Line at Felin Fran (see page 90). The line became known as the Cwmgorse branch, but was only built as far as a nearby colliery. A Peckett 0-6-0 shunts on the branch near Gwaun-cae-Gurwen on 19 May 1958.

The track has now been taken up, but the line was easy to trace in April 2001. There are proposals to use part of the trackbed as a bypass for Gwaun-cae-Gurwen. *N. C. Simmons, courtesy Hugh Davies/TG*

INDEX OF LOCATIONS